LET'S INVESTIGATE

FIRST AID

Published in this edition by Peter Haddock Ltd, Pinfold Lane,
Bridlington, East Yorkshire YO16 5BT

ISBN 0 7105 0969 3

Printed and bound in India

PART ONE

WHAT IS FIRST AID ?

You have probably read exciting stories about children who have rescued their friends from a fire or from drowning. These things, you may think, do not happen in real life, but sometimes they do.

Your friend may rush out into the road without looking and be hit by a car. An ambulance or doctor will take time to get to the spot—valuable time. What can you do in the meantime? Or he may have fallen off his bike and cut his leg badly. How can you help?

It might only be a small thing—your friend has been stung by a wasp while you are playing in the garden. You are the only one around to help—could you?

The help you give someone *immediately,* before more skilled help arrives, is called *first aid,* and in many cases prompt action has saved lives.

It is too late, when an accident happens, to look in a book to find out what to do. Although not everything can be learned from a book, *Let's Investigate First Aid* is a beginning for you, telling you what to do in an emergency, telling you things to practise.

First aid can be a hobby, too, and it is best if you have a friend or group of friends to share it with you. You'll certainly need someone to practise bandaging and the recovery position on, as well as the other things you will learn together.

It is a good idea to keep a special little notebook to jot down things you learn and things that are particularly important to remember.

PART TWO

GOLDEN RULES

There are three main rules for first aid:

1 Do not panic—try to sum up the situation as quickly as possible. (You'd be surprised how many people *do* panic, even adults. This never helps a situation.)

2 First things first—carry out the essentials of first aid.

3 Telephone for help.

Project

Using a telephone

If you are within reach of a private phone in either your own or someone else's house, it is very simple:

1 Pick up the telephone receiver and dial 999 for the fire brigade, the police or the ambulance service. (Unless the accident involves a fire, you will normally require an ambulance only. For a road accident ask for ambulance and police.)

2 The operator will ask you which service you require. Ask for it clearly, saying where you are phoning from. You will then be connected to the appropriate service.

3 Give all the details to the fire brigade/police/ambulance service, including where the accident is, what you think has happened and the telephone number of where you are calling from.

4 Speak slowly and clearly and do not ring off until you hear them ring off.

5 If you are not near a private phone, you can dial 999 from a public telephone box. You do not need any money. All you have to do is pick up the receiver and dial.

You can always ask someone to telephone for you if you are busy attending to the casualty. Just remember to tell them to pass on all the relevant details.

Project

Your doctor's number

Make a note in your notebook of your family doctor's number. Find out if there is a different number after surgery hours.

FIRST THINGS FIRST

Before attending an accident or helping someone who is injured, there are a few things that you should do.

1 If the injury looks serious send immediately for an ambulance or the doctor.

2 Do not put yourself in danger.

3 Try to remain calm and reassuring.

4 If the casualty is conscious, try to find out some information, for example, his or her name, age and any details about what happened. This will help you to treat him or her, or if the patient needs to go to hospital it will help the staff at the hospital.

FIRST AID BOX—YOUR OWN PRIVATE MINI-HOSPITAL

Most of the accidents that happen around you won't be so serious as to need ambulances and hospitals.

It is essential, though, that you have your own 'mini-hospital'—your first aid box. You can always keep it handy at home (well away from the reach of younger brothers and sisters). Whenever you go out on a hike or for any longish outing you can take a few of the most essential items with you in a polythene bag.

Project 

Make your own first aid box

Some of the things in your first aid box can be collected from your own home, and your parents will be able to give you one or two of them. The other things you can buy quite cheaply in a pharmacist's shop, and you can collect them gradually. If you are sharing your hobby with friends you could perhaps all pay something towards the costs or perhaps your parents will contribute some money.

THE BOX

A large, cleaned biscuit or cake tin would make an ideal first aid box. You can label it clearly—or paint it white, then paint *First Aid* in green on the lid.

WHAT YOU NEED IN YOUR BOX

Bandages

- Two triangular bandages. You can make these by cutting up a piece of linen or calico, not less than 1 metre (40 inches) square, diagonally into two pieces. (A triangular bandage has, of course, three sides.)
- Open-weave bandages of various widths, which are obtainable quite cheaply at the pharmacist's.

Dressings

- Several sterilised unmedicated dressings of various sizes.
- Rolls of sticky tape, and one or packets of different sized waterproof dressings.
- An old (but clean) flannel for a cold compress.

Miscellaneous

- Some safety pins, a pair of tweezers and a pair of scissors
- Some distilled water in a plastic bottle.
- A thermometer.
- A small torch.
- A packet of paper tissues and a roll of cotton wool.

Remember: Keep your tin as tidy as possible, so you don't have to turn it inside out to find what you are looking for. Try not to use the things in your tin to practise with. If you do use anything, replace it as soon as possible.

Project

Travelling first aid kit

You can make up a handy little kit in a polythene bag to carry around with you—in your rucksack, bag or pocket. It can contain: a tin of bandages, a triangular bandage, safety pins, paper tissues (a small packet) and/or cotton wool.

PART THREE

SMALL EVERYDAY INJURIES

The following accidents can happen at any time. This is where your first aid box can come in useful.

Project

Cuts

Small cuts on the knee or finger happen all the time. Your friend trips up in the garden or scrapes his hand on the sharp edge of a toy.

Clean the cut with water (do not use soap) and dab dry with cotton wool. Put on a waterproof dressing or, if necessary, a sterile dressing, fixed with tape. Remember not to touch the pad of a waterproof dressing. Use the flaps to apply it to the wound.

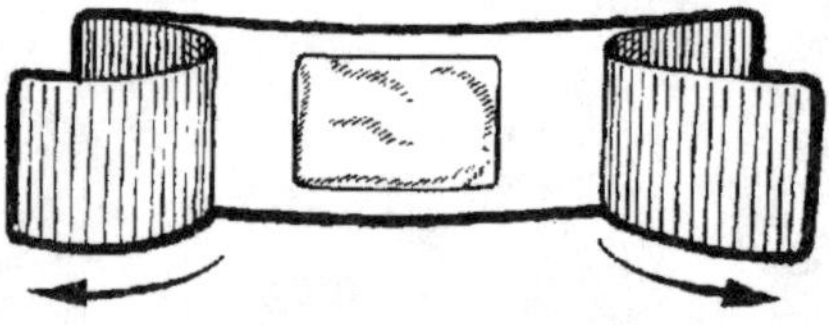

Project

Splinters

Clean the skin around the splinter if it looks dirty. Use a pair of tweezers, passing them through the flame of a match first to sterilise them, to extract the splinter. If it cannot be removed or if it breaks, then seek medical help.

Project

Something in the eye

The first thing a person usually does is to rub his eye—you must stop him doing this, as it makes the irritation worse. You can try several things to try to move the speck of grit or dust into the lower lid where it is easier to remove:

1 Sit the patient in a chair and ask him to lean his head back.

2 Separate the lids with your thumb and forefinger and ask the patient to move his eyeball in each direction. This will help you to locate the foreign body.

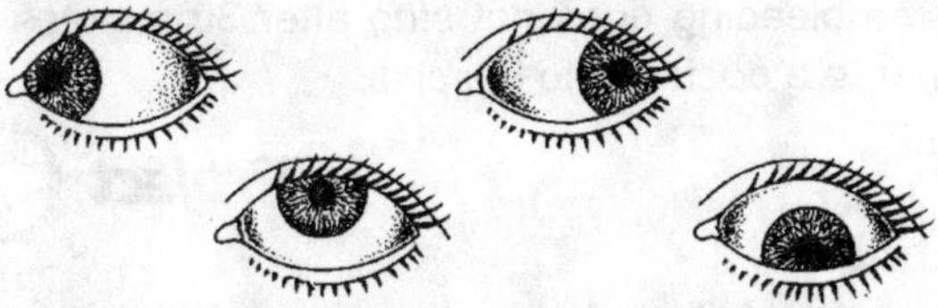

3 If you can see the speck in the lower lid, tell the patient to look up and you can remove the speck with the corner of a hanky or tissue.

4 If the eye feels sore he can use an eye bath (a small egg-cup would do).

5 If it seems that something is embedded in the eye itself, take him to a doctor or hospital as quickly as possible.

Project

Nose bleed

Some people have a tendency to nosebleeds, and if so they take it in their stride and can usually cope. But for someone who has never had a nosebleed it can be quite frightening, and you will need to help.

Sit the patient down, with her head slightly forward, and pinch her nose just below the bony part for about 10 minutes. Ask her to breath through her mouth while you are doing this.

If the bleeding does not stop after 30 minutes then take her to a doctor or to hospital.

Project

Fainting

You can often tell in advance if someone is going to faint.

He goes pale, perhaps breaks out in a cold sweat, sways unsteadily or complains of giddiness and sickness.

If you have warning, take the patient into the fresh air and, if it is summer, into the shade. Loosen tight clothing about the neck, chest and waist.

The quickest and easiest thing to do is to sit the patient down and push his head between his knees—this will allow more blood to go to his head. If he has already fainted, lay him on his back, turn his head to one side and raise his feet higher than his head—you can prop his feet on coats or cushions.

Project

Headache

The best cure for a mild headache is for the sufferer to sit down and take it easy for a while. If the headache is severe, she should lie down and sleep for a while.

Project

Taking the temperature

A persistent headache, perhaps with other symptoms, can show that a person is more seriously unwell—perhaps 'flu or a cold is coming. A reading from a thermometer will confirm this. The normal body temperature is between 36°C (98°F) and 37.2°C (99°F); clinical thermometers mark 36.8°C (98.4°F) as normal. Do not take a person's temperature after he has eaten or drunk, as the food or drink changes the mouth's temperature for a little while. You should always make sure the mercury is shaken down to at least 10°C (50°F) before you use the thermometer.

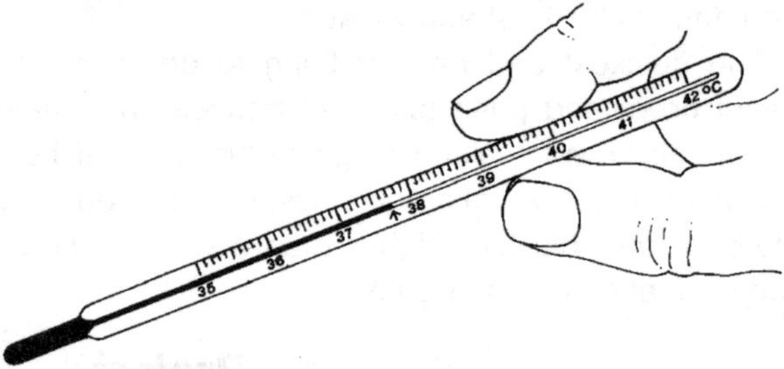

Put the thermometer in the person's mouth, under the tongue, for about half a minute, but ask him not to apply any pressure to the thermometer with his teeth. After you have read the temperature on the thermometer, shake the mercury down again, dip it in disinfectant, wash it in cold water and dry it. (If you are taking a baby's temperature put the thermometer under the armpit.)

If the temperature is 37.7°C (100°F) or over a doctor should be called.

Project 

Choking

You might often come across the situation, especially at meal times, when someone starts to cough and gasps: 'It has gone down the wrong way'. What happens, in fact, is that the food, instead of going down the gullet, or oesophagus, becomes wedged in the windpipe or trachea. The airway becomes blocked and this is why the person chokes.

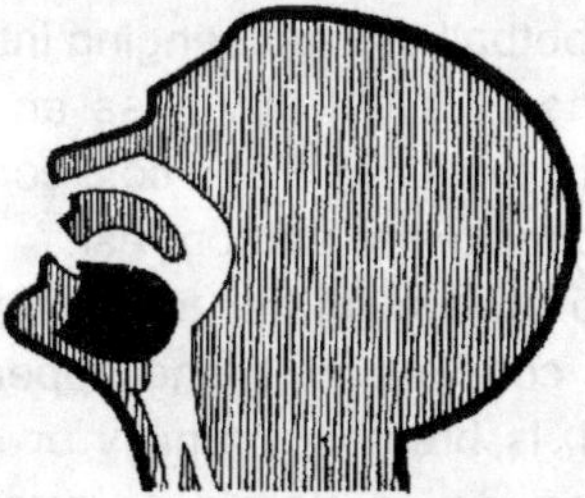

This *can* be serious, but prompt action helps. The aim is to get the piece of food up from the windpipe area.

If the person concerned is a young child, hold him upside down or put him across your knees and give him a few sharp thumps between the shoulder blades.

For an older person, help him to bend forward at the waist. Stand behind him and slap him firmly between the shoulder blades.

If someone swallows a fish bone, this is not normally dangerous. Give him a piece of bread to eat. This will wrap around the bone, which will then be digested with the bread.

If these things bring no success, get the person to a doctor or hospital—*immediately.*

Project

A bump on the head

Knocks on the head can be very frightening—there is such a loud 'crack' that you feel the skull must have split in two. But our skulls are very tough. A normal bump, from a football or from banging into a door, may cause a headache or slight dizziness and often a bruise—but, generally, that is all. Put a cold compress on the affected part and make the person rest.

Keep an eye on her for an hour or two for signs of delayed concussion. If she appears to be confused or forgetful, is breathing rapidly or complaining of feeling sick, then call a doctor or arrange for her to go to hospital.

Project

Black eye

For one reason or another, people tend to regard a black eye as something of a joke. It might be to do with that old song about 'Two lovely black eyes'. But, of course, it is painful and needs as much care as any other accident. A black eye is usually caused by a knock on the forehead or nose. Cover the eye with a cold compress.

Remember: it is essential to seek medical advice with all eye injuries as they may be more serious than they at first appear.

Project

Toothache

Toothache can be miserable—a visit to the dentist is called for in the near future. Meanwhile, you can help by warming a cloth which the patient can hold on the painful side of the jaw.

Project

Hysteria

You might find that certain people, after being upset or frightened—perhaps as the result of an accident or scare—become hysterical. They may laugh or cry or shout in a distraught way.

Your natural instinct would be to comfort the sufferer, especially if he is crying; but you must be firm and reassuring. *Don't give sympathy*—this makes a person in this condition worse. Sit him down or stand him still and handle him gently but firmly to try to shock him out of it.

PRACTICE MAKES PERFECT

When your friends and family know you are keen to learn and practise first aid, get them to come to you if they have minor cuts or bruises. The more practice you can get in treating these complaints the more skilled you will become.

Project

Practise with friends

As well as using any opportunities you have for dealing with real accidents, you and your friends can also practise attending to some of the minor injuries mentioned in this section. You can have fun doing this—but remember, one day a lot may depend on your skill and knowledge, so, at the same time, take your practice seriously.

Project

Equipment for practice

Collect a set of practice equipment and keep it together in a large box or tin.

You will need: pieces of an old sheet for bandages, paper tissues, salt and water (for disinfectant), and an old, clean flannel (for a cold compress).

When you all know what to do, from demonstrations and practice, stage the 'accidents' and 'emergencies' as realistically as you can.

Project

Imitation wounds

If you are practising bandaging cuts or grazes, for example, it is best to have a 'pretend' cut to work on. Here are a few ways you can fake some wounds with your friends.

Grazes: rub a little Vaseline into the skin, add red poster paint or lipstick ('blood') and then a little earth and a few pieces of gravel .

Cuts: grease the skin, then put a flat piece of flesh-coloured Plasticine in place and smooth the edges into the skin. Cut into the Plasticine with a blunt edge and add 'blood'.

Pale face: powder with a little talcum or flour to give the effect of paleness or add a red blusher for a flush.

Burns: grease skin with Vaseline and redden with rouge or lipstick. Drop candle-grease 'blisters' on to a knife and when cool transfer to the 'burn'.

Experiment for yourselves with other ideas for fake wounds—splinters or a black eye, for example. But avoid scaring other people.

Keep all your 'wound' equipment in your practice box. Try out your ideas together so that everyone is used to staged incidents before you spring them on each other.

Project

Have a competition

When you have had some practice, and learned how to deal with minor injuries, you can organise a competition with your friends.

Perhaps you are sharing your hobby with four friends. You can start as the 'judge'. Write, on four pieces of paper, four different injuries. For example—fainting, choking, something in the eye, nosebleed. Fold over the papers so no one can see the writing, and mix them up in your hand. Let each of your friends take one.

One at a time, each person must act out what is on the paper and the others must *diagnose,* or decide, the trouble and deal with it as quickly as possible.

This means that not all of you should try to do the same thing. One can hold the 'patient', another can fetch and carry, and so on. If the injury on the paper said 'a cut' or 'a graze', the 'patient' can have time to make himself up.

This is a chance for you to show your skill as actors and actresses, provided everyone takes it seriously.

PART FOUR

BANDAGING

One of the most useful things you can practise in first aid is bandaging. It is no use waiting until someone is injured to practise your bandaging—you must have the necessary speed and skill first. A clumsy bandage can make someone very uncomfortable. Remember that an injured person is usually anxious, and he likes to feel that whoever looks after him knows what he's doing. The two main types of bandages you will use are the *triangular bandage* and the *roller bandage.*

WHAT IS THE DIFFERENCE BETWEEN A BANDAGE AND A DRESSING?

A *dressing* is material that goes directly over a wound—either an adhesive plaster for a small cut or graze or a sterile dressing for a larger, more serious wound. A *bandage* usually doesn't touch a wound but it can be used for:

- Holding dressings or splints in position.
- To reduce swelling (for example, a sprain).
- Supporting a broken limb.
- To act as padding and protection.
- To give pressure on a dressing and help control bleeding.

TRIANGULAR BANDAGES

One of the most useful and versatile of bandages is the three-cornered one. It's not a bandage that should be left on for weeks to protect a wound (unless it is being used as a sling) but is an excellent temporary protection. You can make some out of old clean sheets for practice.

On the following page you can see the ways in which it can be used.

Opened fully, the triangular bandage can be used to bandage the head, chest, shoulder, elbow, hand, foot and knee—and as a sling.

Folded, as a *broad* or *narrow* bandage, it can be used on the knee or elbow or for an ankle or wrist sprain.

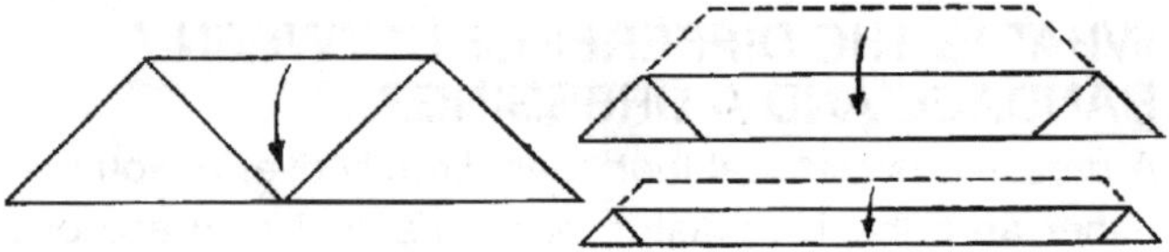

Here are the names of the different parts of the triangular bandage:

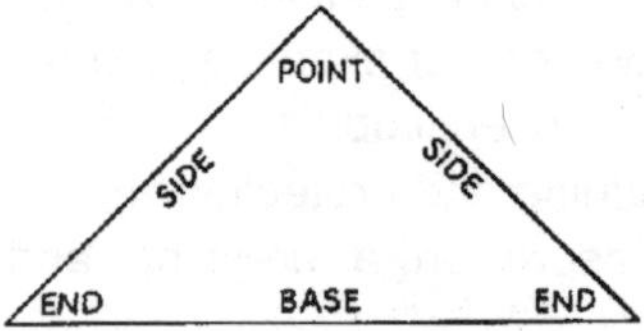

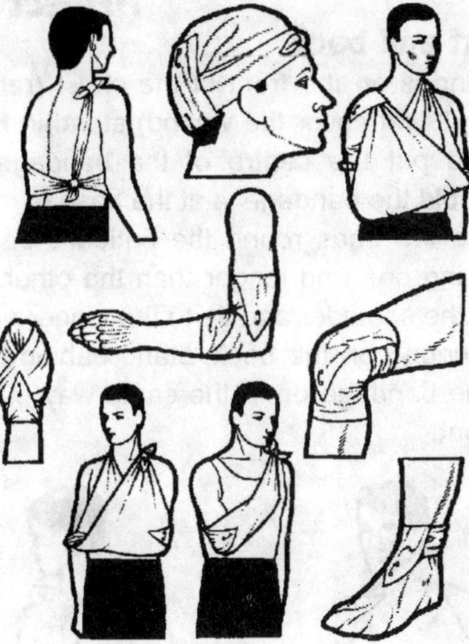

REEF KNOTS

Always use a reef knot when you secure a bandage. It is quite flat, it feels comfortable and will not slip. Left over right . . . right over left. The illustrations below show the correct knot.

Project

The chest and back

If the wound is on the front of the chest (remember, a dressing will first cover the wound) stand in front of the patient and put the centre of the bandage over the dressing. Fold the bandage in at the base to make a firm 'hem'. Take the ends round the patient's back and tie them, leaving one end longer than the other. Bring the point over the shoulder and tie to the longer end.

For a wound on the back, stand behind the patient and put the bandage on in the same way but tying the ends in front.

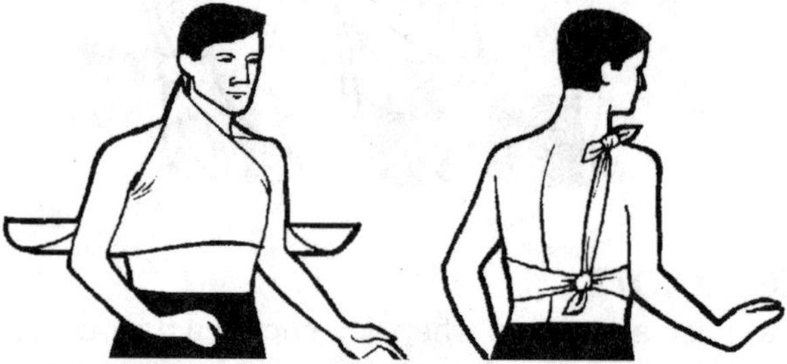

Project

Head

Put the bandage over the patients head with the point hanging down at the back. Tie the ends in front and pin the point over.

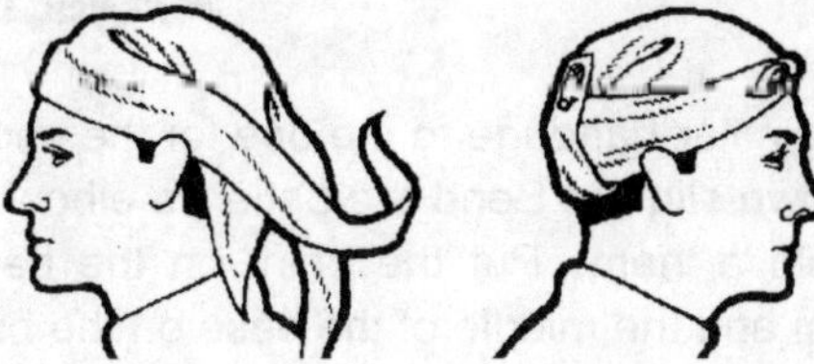

Project

Shoulder

Stand opposite the patient's injured side and put the centre of the bandage on his shoulder so that the point reaches the tip of his ear. Fold a 'hem' along the base, take the ends round the middle of his arm, and cross and tie them on the outer side. Then put on an arm sling (*see* page 33) and turn the point of the shoulder bandage down over the knot of the sling. Draw it tight and pin it.

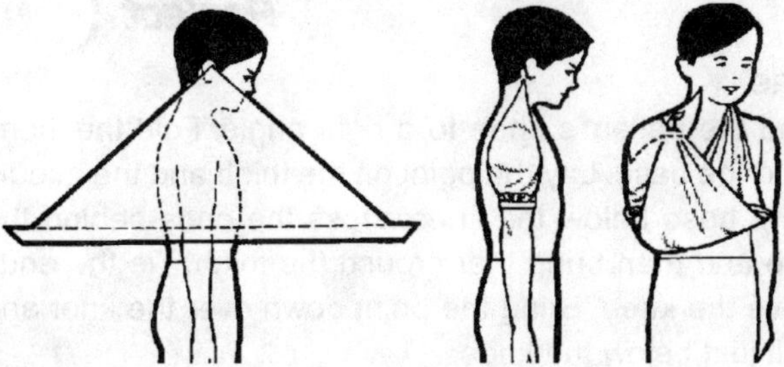

Project

Elbow

This is a similar bandage to the one for the shoulder but moved down slightly. Bend the patient's elbow to a right angle. Fold a 'hem'. Put the point on the back of the upper arm and the middle of the base on the back of the forearm. Cross the ends in front of the elbow, then round the upper arm and tie above the elbow. Bring the point down over the knot and the elbow, and pin.

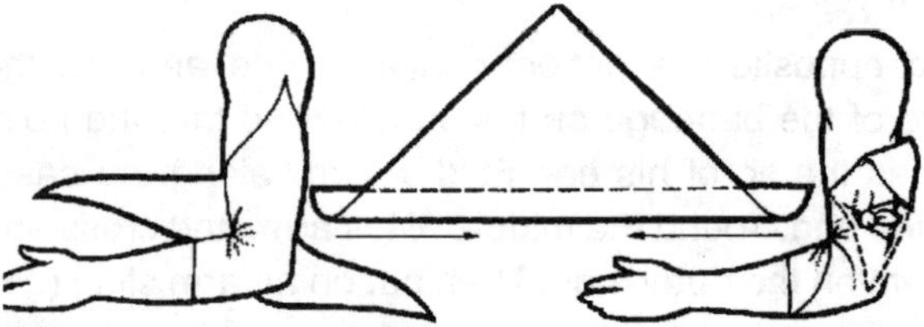

Project

Knee

Bend the patient's knee to a right angle. Fold the 'hem' along the base. Lay the point on the thigh and the middle of the base below the knee; cross the ends behind the knee and then bring them round the thigh. Tie the ends above the knee. Bring the point down over the knot and pin it just below the knee.

If it is painful for the patient to bend her knee or

elbow, use the triangular bandage as a broad or narrow bandage.

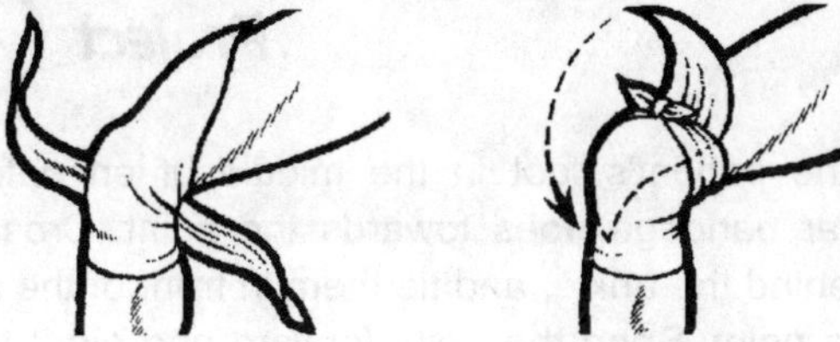

Project

Hand

If a person has injured the back of his hand, put the bandage over the dressing so that the base of the bandage is at the wrist.

Then fold the point over the hand. Make a 'hem' on the base, pass the ends round the wrist, cross them and tie over the point. Fold the point over the knot and pin it to the bandage.

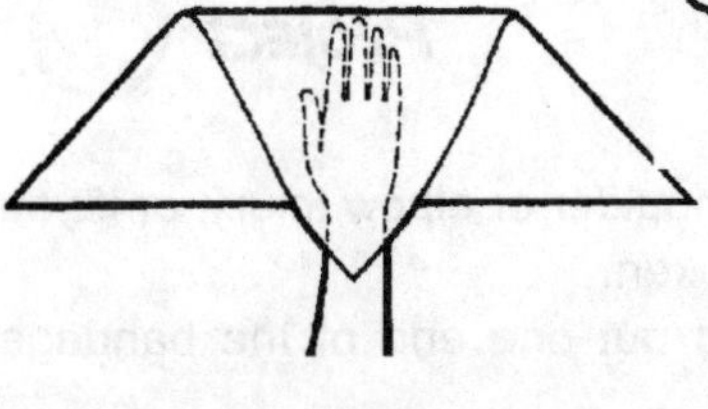

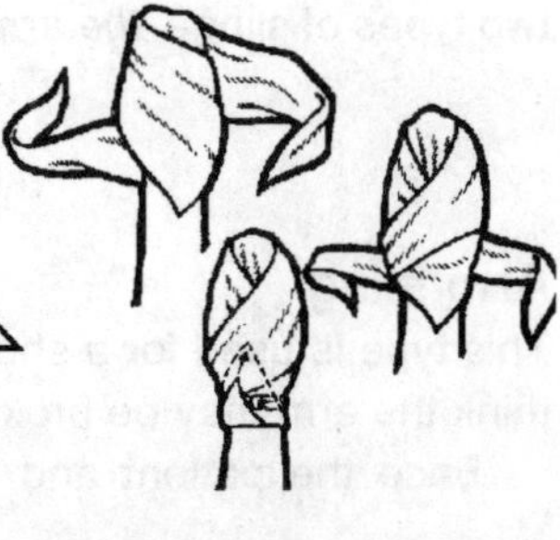

All hand and arm wounds should be supported in a sling (*see* page 33).

Project

Foot

Place the patient's foot in the middle of an unfolded triangular bandage, toes towards the point. Cross the ends behind the ankle, and tie them in front of the ankle over the point. Bring the point forward and pin it to the bandage over the instep.

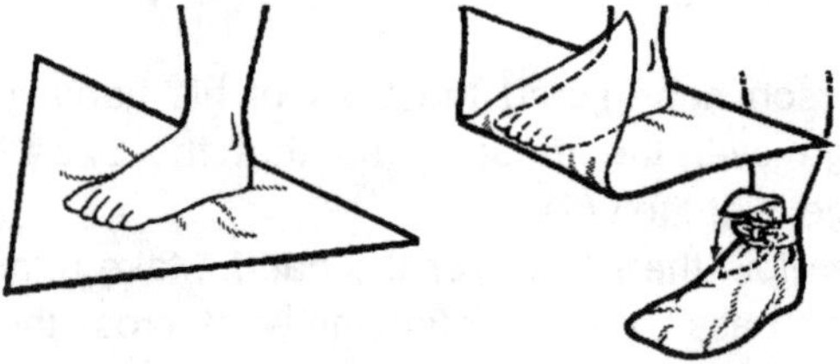

SLINGS

Slings are used to support the arm and hand. There are two types of sling—*the arm sling* and the *triangular sling.*

Project

Arm sling

This type is used for a shoulder or elbow injury, or if you think the arm may be broken.

Face the patient and put one end of the bandage

over his shoulder on the *uninjured side.* The point should be towards the injured side and behind the elbow. Bring the end of the bandage around the patient's neck, so it appears over the shoulder of the injured side. The arm should be just above the waist line and at a right angle. Bring the second end of the bandage up to the first and tie them in the hollow just above the collar bone. Tuck the bandage in to the back of the elbow, bring the point forward and pin it to the front of the bandage.

Project

Triangular sling

This type of sling can be used to keep the hand high if it is bruised or injured, or when you think the collar bone might be broken.

Raise the patient's arm so that the hand rests on the

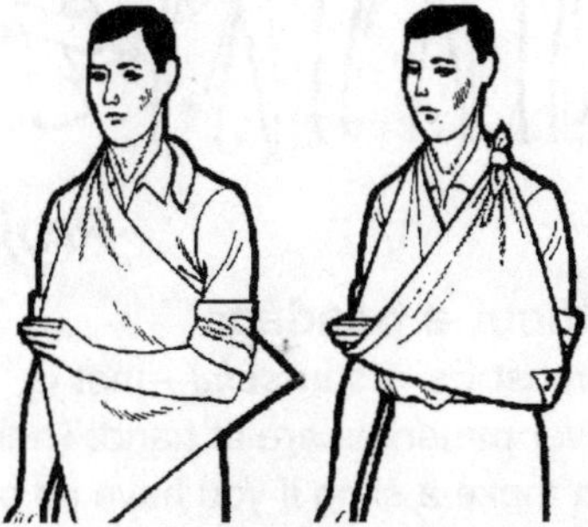

chest with the fingers pointing towards the shoulder. Place the bandage over the forearm with one end over the hand and the point well beyond the elbow. Tuck the base under the arm, carrying the lower end up the back. Tie the ends in a knot in the hollow above the collar bone. Tuck the loose point of the bandage well in between the forearm and the bandage in front. Turn this fold backwards and pin it.

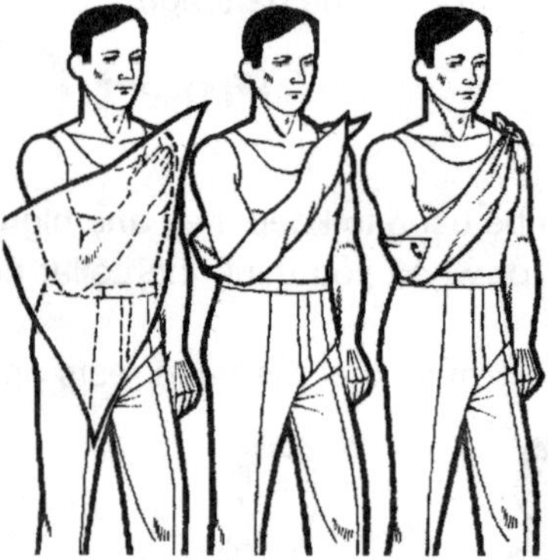

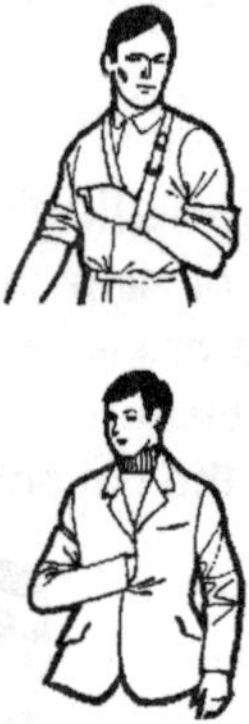

Project

Caught without a bandage

A first aider must be *resourceful*—that is, he can make use of whatever materials are at hand. There are several ways you can make a sling if you have no bandage near. Some are illustrated above. Can you think of others?

Project

Roller bandages

This is another use for old sheets. Cut them up carefully into strips of different widths as you did for your first aid box. Always roll the bandages up again when you have used them. A roller bandage is used for keeping dressings in place and for supporting dislocated joints.

WHY USE A ROLLER BANDAGE INSTEAD OF A TRIANGULAR ONE?

A triangular bandage is only used as a temporary supporting bandage, unless it is used as a sling. If someone has to keep a dressing on a wound for several weeks until it heals, imagine how difficult a triangular bandage would make coping with everyday activities. So a roller bandage is more permanent; and as it must stay in place for a day or more until the dressing underneath is changed, it must be very firm.

You'll need lots of practice, otherwise you'll find the bandage collapsing like a concertina.

Project

Practise roller bandaging

Simple spiral. You can use this bandage on a part of the body that is of even thickness—such as the wrist, ankle or finger.

Reverse spiral. When you are bandaging parts of the

body that get thicker—upper arm, thigh, leg—you will have to do a reverse spiral to keep it in place. As you wind the bandage, you twist it towards you over your thumb. Study the picture and then try it out for yourself.

Figure of eight. This is done in a similar way to winding the narrow and broad triangular bandage, but here you keep repeating the turns. Carry the bandage round the joint, making alternate turns upwards and downwards like the loops of a figure eight. When you have finished, the joint should be firmly and securely covered.

You and your friends will have to be very patient as

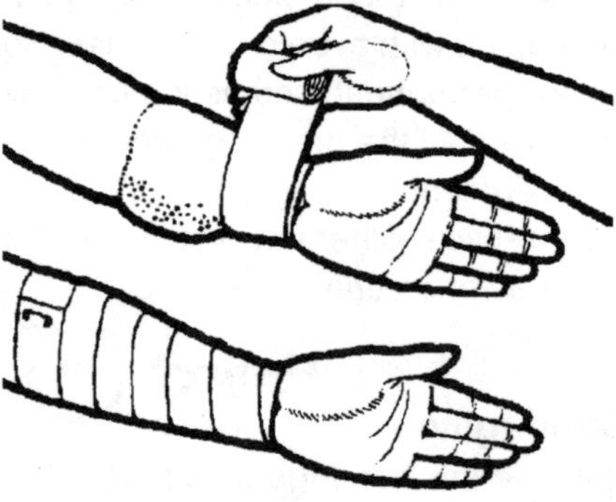

simple spiral

reverse spiral

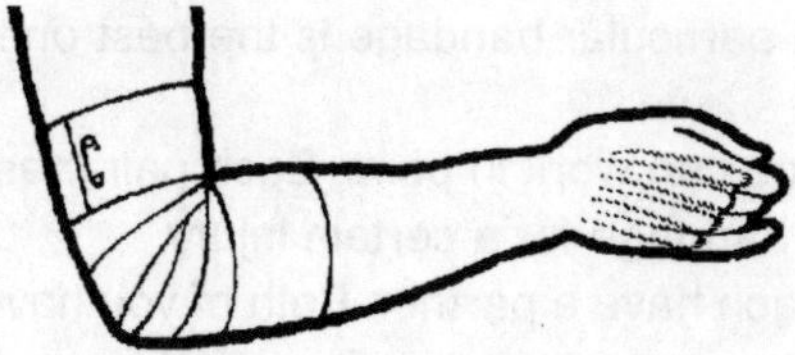
figure of eight

you practise your bandaging on each other. Test each other and keep a list in your notebook of the bandages you really know, like this:

Can do a reef knot	√
Can do two kinds of sling	
Can do a foot bandage	√
Knows different parts of bandage	
Can do a simple spiral	

When you have become expert, you can try some more competitions.

Project

Bandaging competitions

You can organise a competition rather like the one on page 23. Each person has a slip of paper with an injury, *not* a bandage, named on it—for example, 'wound on foot', 'wound on chest', broken collarbone', and so on. In turn, each tells the others what is wrong and they must then decide which particular bandage is the best one to use.

Alternatively, you can work in pairs. Each pair tries to put on the correct bandage for a certain injury.

Or you could each have a partner. Both of you have a slip of paper with the name of a bandage that you must then try on your partner. For example, 'reverse spiral on ankle', 'simple spiral on wrist', or 'triangular sling'.

Divide into teams. Each team makes up a situation for another team. 'You are in the country on a hike, and your friend falls, cutting her finger and spraining her wrist'. Or you can make it more difficult: 'You are by the sea and your friend falls over, stubs her toe, cuts her chest and sprains her ankle. You have on you a couple of large hankies, a tie and a scarf. What can you do to help her?'

Project

Learn how to carry an injured person

Try out these ways of lifting and carrying an injured person for yourself.

Never try to move someone if you think he may have broken his legs, his back or neck, or if he is in severe pain. You could do more harm than good. All the methods shown on this page are useful if someone has hurt or sprained his leg, feels faint, is unconscious or suffering from shock.

Project

More methods of carrying

On the next page you can see a picture of a stretcher. Can you think of ways to *improvise* a stretcher?

Using some of the methods shown on this page it is possible to lift even a heavy person. Try them out with people of different weights.

Can you think of other ways to carry someone?

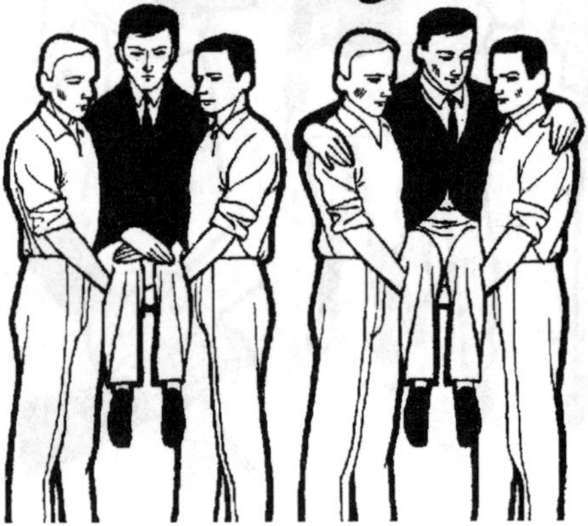

PART FIVE

BROKEN BONES

A broken bone is called a *fracture.* Although our bones are normally quite tough, a heavy kick or an awkward fall can cause a bone to break.

You should take great care if you suspect that someone has broken a bone.

He should not be moved except by a doctor or an ambulance team, who will see that no further harm is done.

Do not rush to help someone to his feet if he has had a fall. It's better to let him lie where he is for a moment (unless he is obviously unhurt of course) and try to find out what is wrong.

Project

How to tell if a bone is broken

1 Severe pain at the fracture and tenderness around it.

2 Swelling around the area of the fracture caused by bleeding in the tissues.

3 A broken limb may look awkward or 'different' if you compare it with a sound one. It may appear to be misshapen or in an unusual position.

4 Loss of movement of the limb.

Project

What to do

Disturb the broken limb as little as possible.

Treat the person for shock (*see* page 52).

Keep the broken bone immobilised.

Project

Broken leg

You can bandage a broken leg to the sound one for support, but always remember, *the patient must not be moved.*

Project

Broken arm or collar bone

You can put a sling on a broken arm without disturbing it too much. (You learned this on page 33.)

You could then move the injured person to hospital by car, but if he seems unwell, it's best to leave him to be taken by ambulance.

Project

A broken bone piercing the skin

If the broken bone shows through the wound, there is great danger of infection. Move the limb as little as possible but lightly cover the wound with a sterile dressing or a clean pad of material. Apply more padding around the dressing, building it up in layers, before gently bandaging the dressing in place. The aim is to build up the padding around the dressing so that there isn't any pressure on the bone. Lose no time in calling an ambulance.

IT IS BEST NOT TO GIVE ANYTHING TO DRINK

If the injury is serious, the person may need an anaesthetic on arrival at the hospital. An anaesthetic is usually given when there is nothing in the stomach.

WHAT DOES A BROKEN BONE LOOK LIKE?

If you had X-ray eyes, this is what you would see under the skin. There are three main types of fracture—simple (closed), compound (open) and complicated.

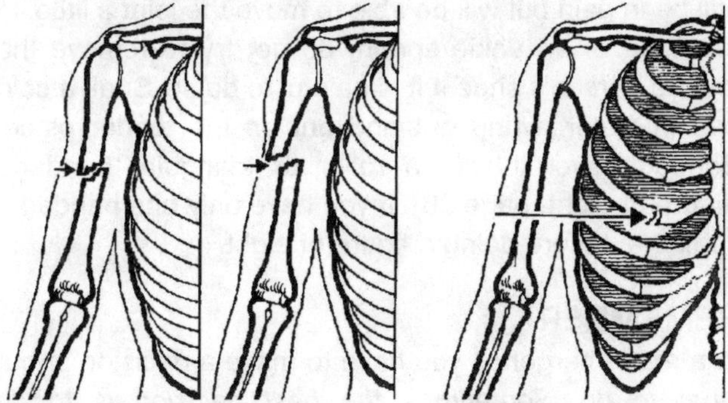

simple *compound* *complicated*

BROKEN RIBS

This *can* be serious if the rib punctures the lung. Keep the person very still if he complains of pains in the chest—this can indicate cracked or broken ribs.

SPRAINS

A sprain happens when the ligaments or tissues round a joint are pulled or torn. (A ligament is a short band of tough, flexible tissue binding bones together.)

The most common places for sprains are round the wrist and ankle. A sprain may seem very similar to a fracture, so if you are in any doubt at all, treat as a fracture.

In the case of a mild sprain, the injured person will still be in pain but will be able to move the joint a little. In the case of an ankle sprain, do not try to remove the injured person's shoe if it is painful to do so. Soak a cold pad in water, wring out and put on the tender place. Bandage over it with a roller or triangular bandage (figure of eight, page 36). If you have only one bandage, soak that before doing a figure of eight.

REMEMBER

In a real emergency you have to make a decision about what to do. *Sometimes the best decision is to do nothing*—or very little—unless you are absolutely certain. Be glad if someone older and more experienced in first aid is there to take charge, and give all the help you can. Whether it is telephoning, fetching or carrying for someone else, you can still make a very valuable contribution. And all the time you are learning more and more by watching.

PART SIX

MORE SERIOUS INJURIES

So far, you have mostly learned how you can deal with minor injuries that are likely to happen at any time. The emergencies in this section you are not so likely to meet, but they are the ones where it is extremely important to know what to do, because lives may depend on it. If you wish to learn life-saving procedures such as artificial respiration and chest compression, then it is possible to attend first aid classes run by the British Red Cross Association, the St Andrew's Ambulance Association (in Scotland), and the St John Ambulance Association. More details can be found on page 67.

BAD BLEEDING

A very deep cut needs more treatment than a bandage or dressing. Heavy bleeding will occur if an artery or vein has been cut. It is especially likely to happen on a place like the inside of the arm where there is not much fat protecting the veins. Heavy bleeding seems frightening, but it can always be controlled.

1 Do not waste time washing the cut.

2 You will need lots of dressings. Press *hard* on the cut with a pad. If the blood soaks through, do not take the old pad away but cover with another and, if needed, another.

3 Bandage round the pads to keep them firm. Keep the limb—that is, the arm or leg—raised.

IF THERE IS GLASS OR METAL IN THE CUT

Do not press on the wound—it will press the object in further and cause more damage. Cover the wound and *surround* it with bandages.

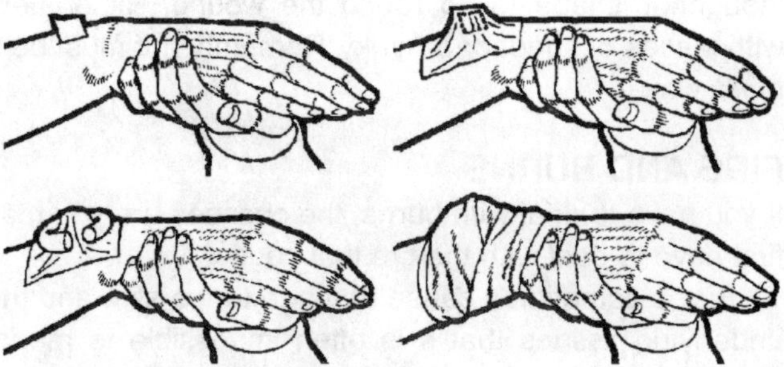

NO FIRST AID BOX WITH YOU?

The sterile dressings in your first aid box are ideal for covering a bad wound, but what happens if you are away from home with no first aid box handy?

Use the inside of a clean hanky, a clean towel or clean paper tissues. If there's nothing better, a tie or belt can be tied over the hanky or towel. Can you think of other ways?

Project

Practise stopping bleeding

1 You can use your 'imitation wound' kit again and make up a large wound on, for example, someone's arm. Practise pressing on the pads and bandaging firmly. Can you think of a way of, making an object seem to stick out of the 'wound'?

2 Can you think of a way to make a bandage into a 'doughnut' shape to go round the wound. Experiment with pieces of sheet or a hanky. Remember, it must be a *quick* way.

FIRE AND BURNS

If you have to deal with burns, the chances are you may first have to deal with the fire that caused them.

Burns sometimes cause damage to the skin and the underlying tissues that it is often impossible to mend. Quick action can prevent someone from being badly burned.

House on fire

If part of the house catches alight, get everyone out immediately. Close all the windows and doors you can. This cuts off the draught which boosts the flames.

If you can do so without any risk, throw basins of water over the fire. Or you can smother it under a rug, mat or curtains. If an electrical appliance bursts into flames—for example, the TV set—pull out the plug, or switch it off at the mains.

A frying pan fire

This looks serious but is easily checked if you do not panic. Throw a damp cloth or pan-lid over the flames and smother. *Do not* throw water on this kind of fire. Water spreads fat fires.

If a person's clothes catch fire

A person whose clothes are alight—perhaps through standing too near an open fire—will panic and nearly always run as if trying to escape the flames.

You must throw him to the floor and wrap him in a rug, mat or blanket, or even a heavy overcoat, to smother the flames.

If you are trapped by fire

Try to escape through a ground floor window.

Otherwise, close the doors and windows on the way to an upstairs room overlooking the street. Close the door of the room and seal the bottom of the door with a carpet or rug.

When the door is closed, open a window and shout for help. *Wait by the window until the fire brigade arrives.*

If there is thick smoke, keep your head near the floor—the air is clearer there. Get others to lie on the floor while waiting. A wet hanky in front of the mouth and nose will help to stop you coughing.

BURNS

Severe burns will blister almost immediately, and you must be careful not to break the blisters. Do not try to remove burnt clothing or anything that is sticking to the wound—this may tear the skin. Do not use adhesive dressings or cotton wool to cover the burn as they might damage the affected skin and tissues. Do not apply ointment, sprays or butter to the wound.

Hand and forearm burns. Immerse the burn in cold water, or hold under gently running cold water.

For all burns. If possible, remove any constricting clothing and jewellery near the burn before any swelling occurs. Cover the area with a sterile dressing, or a piece of clean linen.

For a really bad burn which has damaged the tissues below the surface of the skin, simply cover the wound lightly and leave for the doctor to deal with.

WHAT IS THE DIFFERENCE BETWEEN A BURN AND A SCALD ?

A *burn* is caused by dry heat—fire, hot metal, sun.
A *scald* is caused by wet heat—boiling water, steam, hot cooking fat. Always treat scalds in the same way as burns.

ELECTRIC SHOCKS

If you see or discover someone knocked out because he has touched the live wire of an electric plug, or something similar, be very careful. Do not rush to pull him away.

1 Cut off the current at the mains, pull out the plug, or turn off the switch at the socket.

2 If this is not possible, you must get the casualty away from the live wire.

3 *Never* touch the casualty without taking suitable precautions—the shock can pass through him to you.

4 Pull or push the person away with an object made of rubber, glass, wood, silk, cloth or paper (none of these things conduct electricity). For example, use a walking stick, but not an umbrella which has metal spokes.

If your shoes are not rubber-soled, stand on a rubber mat or a pile of old newspapers or magazines.

Project

Acting

By this time, you are probably becoming quite an expert at staging accidents. You can try out several on the theme of fire.

With your friends, take turns in rolling each other in rugs or blankets.

Always remember that while it can be great fun to act out these situations, all the time you are becoming more and more used to thinking quickly and dealing with emergencies.

A few of you might like to make up a short play about a fire in a house—what steps you would take, and so on—to act in front of your parents and friends. With this in mind, you practise even more carefully.

SHOCK

In a serious accident, many people suffer from shock. This is not the same as getting an electric shock but the two things link up. Whenever there is severe pain, and injuries from which a lot of blood has been lost, the body has received a shock—and suffers from it.

Always assume that someone involved in an accident is suffering from shock, even if he seems to carry on as normal.

Watch for these signs:

- The skin becomes pale, cold and clammy and the breathing is shallow.
- The pulse is rapid and feeble.
- The sufferer may complain of feeling sick, weak and giddy.
- If you think that somebody suffering from shock then it is vital that you summon medical help as quickly as possible.

Lay the sufferer down on his back and place his head to one side. Raise his legs from the ground and support them by placing folded blankets or coats under his feet. Keep him still and warm, and cover him with a coat or blanket, tucking it snugly round his feet.

Give him plenty of air and plenty of reassurance. Let him rest.

Now you will always treat for shock at the same time as treating other injuries, so it becomes rather like a crossword puzzle.

Remember: Broken legs should not be raised, even if treating for shock.

Remember: Do not give any liquids if you think a person will eventually need an anaesthetic.

In first aid there are lots of things to think of.

UNCONSCIOUSNESS

Unconsciousness can result from an interruption of the supply of blood or oxygen to the brain, caused by damage to the brain, such as a blow to the head, or an illness, such as diabetes or epilepsy. Somebody who is unconscious will look as if he is sleeping but will not wake up if you speak to him or touch him.

When somebody is unconscious there is a danger that he will choke—his tongue might slip back and block the passage of air or he might be sick.

If you are attending somebody who is unconscious you must summon help immediately—it is almost certain that he will need to be seen by a doctor.

Check inside the casualty's mouth to make sure that there is nothing to block the airway—if there is, then remove it. Loosen clothing around the neck, chest and waist.

Place the casualty in the recovery position:

1 Kneel beside the patient and open the airway by lifting the chin up and tilting the head. The arm nearest you should be placed at right angles to the body, with the elbow bent and the palm uppermost.

2 Bring the other arm across the patient's body and place his hand against his cheek. Hold the arm in this position.

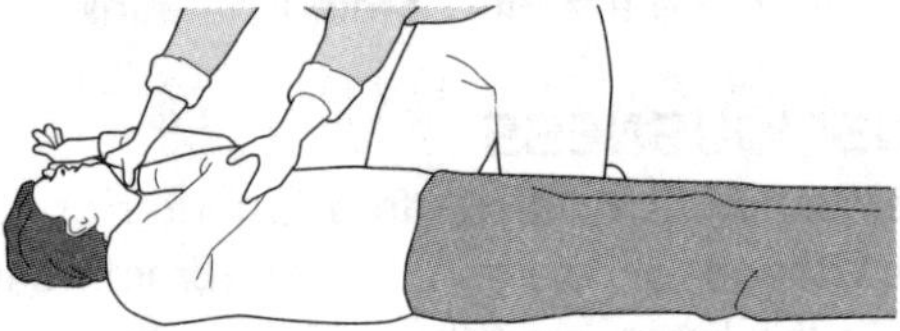

3 With your other hand, firmly grasp the far thigh and pull the knee up and towards you. Continue pulling on the thigh until the patient is on his side with his hand still under his cheek.

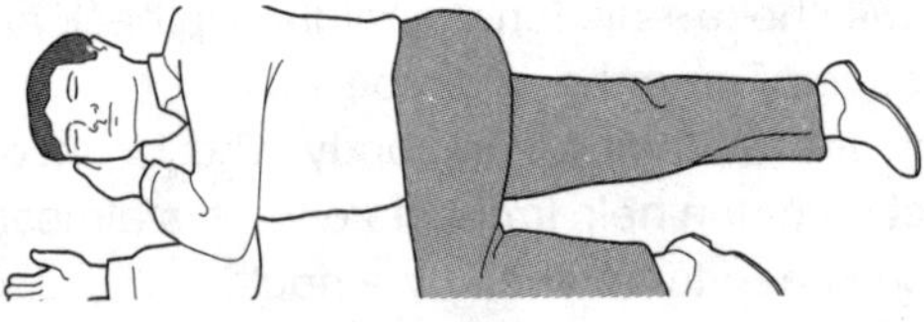

4 Adjust the hand position and tilt the head back again if necessary to ensure that the airway remains open. The hand should keep the head in the correct position.

5 The upper leg should be bent so that the hip and the knee are both at right angles.

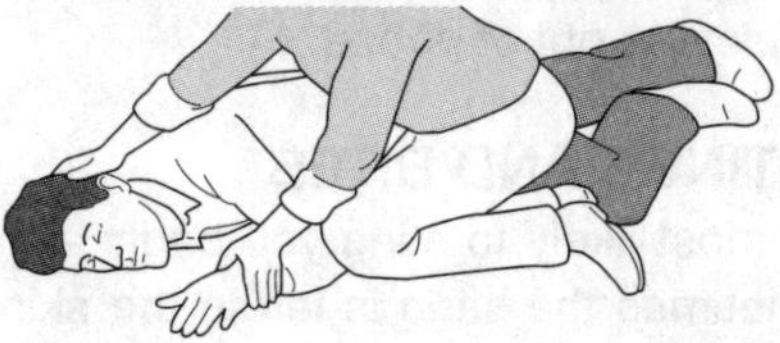

PART SEVEN

SUMMER FIRST AID

In this section you will find out about some accidents that are more likely to happen in fine weather, when you are camping or playing out of doors.

INSECT STINGS AND BITES

The insects most likely to sting you badly are bees and wasps. Sometimes the sting is left in the skin, and you can remove it with a pair of tweezers, taking care not to squeeze the poison sac.

You must learn two rules for treatment—the way you treat the sting site depends on whether it was a bee or wasp that did the stinging. Normally this will not be difficult, as the victim usually sees the culprit.

A bee sting should be treated with a cold compress which will reduce swelling and pain.

A wasp sting should be cleaned with soap and water or with sterile wipes.

WINDING

This is caused by a knock in the stomach, or abdomen, which seems to blow all the breath from your body. This often happens in games out of doors.

Lay the winded person down, draw up his knees and

massage his stomach. Keep him lying down until he feels better.

STITCH

A 'stitch', or pain in the side, often happens while you are running or during any violent exercise, particularly when the runner or 'athlete' is out of training. It is really a violent spasm of the muscle fibres. If the person is not quickly made better by stopping the exercise, give him a sip or two of warm liquid (cold will do) and rub his side gently.

CRAMP

This is caused through a sudden contraction of the muscles, usually when the body is chilled. Swimming will often cause it, and it attacks the leg or stomach muscles. The cramped parts need massage and warmth. Some people get it more than others, and they should be particularly careful when swimming.

WATER RESCUE

Never risk your own safety by trying to swim or wade to somebody in deep water or strong currents. Try to summon help as quickly as possible and then look for objects that you can throw from land to reach the victim, such as a rope or a long pole.

Always remember that it is possible to drown in very shallow water so you should always be extra careful when small children are near water. Always make sure that somebody is in attendance if they are in the bath or playing in a paddling pool and make sure that the water is emptied away once they have finished.

To ensure your own safety do not swim alone and do not swim immediately after eating a meal as this may lead to cramps.

Project

Life-saving

If you are keen to be a stronger swimmer and to learn water rescue, find out from your local swimming baths what courses are available. The Royal Life-Saving Society has special tests, and you can win a medal to show you have learned techniques of life-saving.

SUNBURN

People vary in how much sun they can take without burning. Generally speaking, fair or red-headed people tend to burn more because of the sensitivity of their fair skin.

The burned area of the skin will be sore and red—especially across bony parts like the shoulders. Always ask the patient to move out of direct sunlight and into shade. If the sunburn is quite mild then rub in some calamine lotion or after-sun cream. If these are not available then gently sponge the affected area with cool water. If the sunburn is severe then it should be treated in the same way as any other burn.

But prevention is better than cure—no matter what skin type you are, always use a sunblock. If you have fair skin expose yourself to the sun for a short time only. If you are on a beach where there is no shade, then make sure that you have hat and some clothing that you can put on to protect yourself.

Always apply sunblock before and after you have been swimming—the water-resistant qualities of sunblock cream does not last very long and wet skin burns more easily.

SUNSTROKE

If your body gets over-heated you can become quite ill. A person with sunstroke will probably be red, have a headache, and feel dizzy and sick. He may even pass out. His temperature may be raised, and his pulse will be strong and rapid.

1 Take him into the shade—preferably indoors.
2 Cool him down by removing his clothing and sponging him with cool water, or wrap him in a wet sheet.
3 Give him plenty of cool drinks. Dissolve a small spoonful of salt in each drink—the body loses a lot of salt when it sweats and this helps to replace it.
4 Keep checking the patient's temperature. When the temperature is down to 37.8°C stop the treatment.

5 Let him rest and sleep for a day or more. Call a doctor to see him.

SNAKE BITES

It is very rare for anyone in this country to get a bad snake bite, but it is worth mentioning all the same.

The only poisonous snake in Britain is the adder, or viper, and even then it will not attack you unless you happen to tread on it by mistake.

If someone is bitten:

1 Send for a doctor at once.

2 Tie a bandage (or handkerchief or tie) around the bite on the side of the wound nearest the heart. This stops the poison spreading round the bloodstream.

You have probably all seen dramatic films where the hero sucks out the snake venom and spits it away. *This is not advisable.* Wash the wound thoroughly,

3 Treat the person for shock.

Project

Snakes

Find out the most common snakes in Britain and where they are found. Find out what the adder looks like, so you don't panic needlessly.

Draw sketches in your notebook.

PART EIGHT

HOW NOT TO NEED FIRST AID

This is the last section in the book but by no means the least important. In fact, in some ways it is probably the most important part.

You have had, hopefully, enjoyment from practising and learning first aid, but you would probably agree that it would be better if we didn't need to use our knowledge because there were no accidents.

'It was an accident', people often say, sounding as if nothing could have stopped it and it was sheer bad luck. But the saddest thing is that an incident we call an accident often happens through carelessness and need not have happened at all.

ACCIDENTS AT HOME

'Safe as houses' we say, and we should feel secure and safe in our homes. But more accidents happen in the home every year than anywhere else—even more than on the roads. Why could this be?

Fire

Fire is a major cause of accidents. Always make sure that a real open fire is never left unattended without a fireguard in place. For electric and gas fires make sure that the area around the fire is kept clear of the many household items made of flammable material that can catch light very easily.

Electric plugs and switches

Never touch electrical fittings with wet hands. One of the most dangerous things to do is to stand in the bath and reach out to switch the light on or off. Do not try to fiddle with faulty plugs or the electric socket yourself.

Young children and babies

Young children and babies like to explore, touch and taste everything. Although it is one of the ways they learn about life, we must protect them from learning the hard way. Young children do not realise the dangers, so you must be on the look-out for them.

Medicines

All medicines should be kept out of the reach of young children—preferably locked in a special cabinet. Other poisonous or dangerous things include bleach, cleaning or lighter fluids and ink, and these should also be kept in a safe place out of the reach of children. Remember never to transfer medicines or other liquids into a bottle that has previously contained, say, orangeade. It would be an added incentive to a young child to taste the contents.

Kitchenware

Sharp knives should also be kept away from young children. Saucepans standing on a cooker should always have their handles turned *inwards* and not jutting out over the edge—a child may reach up, pull the handle and empty the scalding contents over himself. Look out, too, for badly made toys with sharp edges.

If possible, tablecloths should not overlap the table if a young child is in the house. He may tug at the cloth and turn the items on the table over himself.

Project

Check your own home

Make a tour of your house or flat, notebook in hand, and check on anything likely to be dangerous.

Do the electric fittings look safe, or are there bare wires showing?

Is there a fireguard in the house?

Are there any loose rugs?

Are the medicines kept in a safe place?

If you do find any dangers, see how they could be put right and made safe.

OUT OF DOORS

Although you have learned that most accidents happen in the home, there are still many dangerous situations that can arise out of doors.

ON THE ROADS

One of the main places for accidents is on the road. You can never take enough care on the road. Never dash out without looking—that is obvious—but do you always remember to do your 'kerb-drill'—look right, look left, look right again before crossing? Use the pedestrian crossing or traffic lights, if you can—and do not feel too important to make use of your school crossing warden.

Remember—just because you step on to a zebra crossing, cars do not stop automatically. You must give an approaching motorist time to see you and slow down before you step on to the crossing. When you do cross, do not run.

Get off a bus only at the proper stopping place. If you step off at traffic lights, for example, and the bus is in the middle lane, it's quite likely that a car will be coming up on the inside lane. Or the bus may start to move and you will be jolted off.

Do you own a bicycle? Be quite sure you know all the proper signals to use when you are cycling in traffic. Regularly check your lights, brakes and bell to make sure that they are working properly.

Always ensure that you wear bright clothing so that you can be seen easily. If you are cycling in the dark or in bad weather, make sure that you are wearing a reflector belt or some strips of reflector material applied to your clothing.

Project

Know your own area

Look around your own neighbourhood and see where the danger spots are on some of the main roads.

Which are specially dangerous places to cross? Why are they dangerous?

Study your route to school and be aware of the danger spots.

Is there an accident 'black spot' in your town? Why is it so dangerous at that particular spot?

Project

Poisonous berries

Do you know which wild fruits are safe to eat, and which are not? Make some drawings and notes in your notebook. Know which berries are *safe* to eat—blackberries, raspberries and bilberries, for example—and what they look like.

As a general rule—never eat any berries unless you are *certain* what they are. If you come across some you don't know, make a sketch and look them up in a book when you get home.

Project

Mushrooms and toadstools

Some mushrooms are safe to eat—toadstools are

poisonous. Can you tell the difference? Again, it is better to be safe than sorry. So always check with a knowledgeable adult if you aren't sure.

PART NINE

LEARNING MORE

In this book we have covered some of the most basic first aid techniques, but it is a large subject and you may feel that you would like to know more. The British Red Cross Society, the St John Ambulance Association, and the St Andrew's Ambulance Association all operate groups specifically for young people that offer training and activities.

The **British Red Cross Society** runs a youth programme that offers the opportunity to develop skills in a wide range of social and health-related areas. You can become a member at the age of five and receive free training in first aid and rescue techniques, and in communication and leadership skills. You will have the chance to meet and help other young people in your community through the Youth Action Teams, which are led by the young members themselves.

The British Red Cross Society currently has over 18,000 youth and younger members enjoying the chance to learn and develop through its training programmes. To find out more contact the Youth Officer at your local branch—you will find the telephone number in your local directory.

The **St John Ambulance Association** (in England

and Wales) and the **St Andrew's Ambulance Association** (in Scotland) run the Badgers and the Cadets. If you are aged between six and ten you can join the Badger Set which offers the chance to learn and practise first aid, learn road safety, develop new hobbies and interests, enjoy special trips and competitions and make new friends.

If you are aged ten and eighteen the Cadets offers you the opportunity to develop your first aid and leadership skills, to take up new challenges, learn how to deal with emergencies and represent the St John Ambulance or St Andrew's Ambulance Associations at major events.

The Three Cross Award also offers the chance to learn more about first aid and welfare. Originally designed for use in schools, this three-part training programme can be run through the Girl Guide and the Scout Associations.

To find out more about the St John Ambulance Association look in your telephone directory for the number of you local branch. For the St Andrew's Ambulance Association, contact the headquarters in Glasgow on 0141-332-4031.

LET'S INVESTIGATE!

Titles in this series:

1 Making Musical Instruments
2 Conjuring
3 Fossil Hunting
4 Being an Inventor
5 First Aid
6 Mapping the Night Sky
7 Ponds and Aquariums
8 Your Dog
9 Your Cat
10 Small Pets
11 Collecting
12 Painting in Watercolours
13 Tracing your Family Tree
14 The Weather
15 Drawing